TSUBASA

CLAMP

TRANSLATED AND ADAPTED BY
Anthony Gerard

LETTERED BY
Dana Hayward

tanoshimi

Published in the United Kingdom by Tanoshimi in 2006

1 3 5 7 9 10 8 6 4 2

This is a work of fiction. Names, characters, places and incidents are the products of the author's imagination or are used fictitiously. Any resemblance to actual events, locales or persons, living or dead, is entirely coincidental.

First published in Japan in 2003 by Kodansha Ltd., Tokyo.

Published by arrangement with Kodansha Ltd., Tokyo and with Del Rey, an imprint of Random House Inc., New York

Tanoshimi
The Random House Group Limited
20 Vauxhall Bridge Road, London, SW1V 2SA

Random House Australia (Pty) Limited
20 Alfred Street, Milsons Point, Sydney
New South Wales 2061, Australia

Random House New Zealand Limited
18 Poland Road, Glenfield
Auckland 10, New Zealand

Random House (Pty) Limited
Isle of Houghton, Corner of Boundary Road & Carse O'Gowrie
Houghton 2198, South Africa

Random House Publishers India Private Limited
301 World Trade Tower, Hotel Intercontinental Grand Complex,
Barakhamba Lane, New Delhi 110 001, India

Random House Group Limited Reg. No 954009

www.tanoshimi.tv
www.randomhouse.co.uk

A CIP catalogue record for this book is available from British Library

Papers used by Random House
are natural, recyclable products made from wood grown in sustainable forests.
The manufacturing processes conform to the enviromental regulations of the country of origin.

ISBN 9780099504139 (from Jan 2007)
ISBN 0 09 950413 8

Printed and bound in Germany by GGP Media GmbH, Pößneck

Translator and Adaptor - Anthony Gerrad
Lettering - Dana Hayward

Contents

Tsubasa crosses over with *xxxHOLiC*. Although it isn't necessary to read *xxxHOLiC* to understand the events in *Tsubasa*, you'll get to see the same events from different perspectives if you read both!

Honorifics Explained

Throughout the Tanoshimi Manga books, you will find Japanese honorifics left intact in the translations. For those not familiar with how the Japanese use honorifics, and more important, how they differ from English honorifics, we present this brief overview.

Politeness has always been a critical facet of Japanese culture. Ever since the feudal era, when Japan was a highly stratified society, use of honorifics – which can be defined as polite speech that indicates relationship or status – has played an essential role in the Japanese language. When addressing someone in Japanese, an honorific usually takes the form of a suffix attached to one's name (example: "Asuna-san"), or as a title at the end of one's name or in place of the name itself (example: "Negi-sensei," or simply "Sensei!").

Honorifics can be expressions of respect or endearment. In the context of manga and anime, honorifics give insight into the nature of the relationship between characters. Many translations into English leave out these important honorifics, and therefore distort the "feel" of the original Japanese. Because Japanese honorifics contain nuances that English honorifics lack, it is our policy at Tanoshimi not to translate them. Here, instead, is a guide to some of the honorifics you may encounter in Tanoshimi Manga.

-san: This is the most common honorific, and is equivalent to Mr., Miss, Ms., Mrs., etc. It is the all-purpose honorific and can be used in any situation where politeness is required.

-sama: This is one level higher than "-san." It is used to confer great respect.

-dono: This comes from the word "tono," which means "lord." It is even a higher level than "-sama," and confers utmost respect.

-kun: This suffix is used at the end of boys' names to express familiarity or endearment. It is also sometimes used by men among friends, or when addressing someone younger or of a lower station.

-chan: This is used to express endearment, mostly toward girls. It is also used for little boys, pets, and even among lovers. It gives a sense of childish cuteness.

Bozu: This is an informal way to refer to a boy, similar to the English term "kid."

Sempai: This title suggests that the addressee is one's "senior" in a group or organization. It is most often used in a school setting, where underclassmen refer to their upperclassmen as "sempai." It can also be used in the workplace, such as when a newer employee addresses an employee who has seniority in the company.

Kohai: This is the opposite of "-sempai," and is used toward underclassmen in school or newcomers in the workplace. It connotes that the addressee is of lower station.

Sensei: Literally meaning "one who has come before," this title is used for teachers, doctors, or masters of any profession or art.

-[blank]: Usually forgotten in these lists, but perhaps the most significant difference between Japanese and English. The lack of honorific means that the speaker has permission to address the person in a very intimate way. Usually, only family, spouses, or very close friends have this kind of permission. Known as *yobisute*, it can be gratifying when someone who has earned the intimacy starts to call one by one's name without an honorific. But when that intimacy hasn't been earned, it can also be very insulting.

RESERVoir CHRoNiCLE
TSUBASA

ツバサ

RESERVoir CHRoNiCLE

Chapitre.6

Strength of the Heart

GWOO
OOOOO
A KUDAN THAT CAN WIELD FIRE...
MINE WORKS WATER AND YOURS, FIRE.
THIS WILL BE INTERESTING!

GYAAAAH
KA PAAH
ZYOOOOO
DOOH

I'M SHÔGO ASAGI.
YOU?
.....
SYAORAN.
SSSHHHH
I LIKE YOUR STYLE.
SSSHHHHH

SHÔGO, THE COPS!
YAAHH!
AND IT WAS JUST GETTING GOOD.
SIGH
COME ON, YA BASTARDS!
LET'S GET OUTTA HERE!
FOWOOO !!
HOOOSH
HOOSH
HOOSH
HOOSH
HOOSH
NEXT TIME WE MEET, WE'LL HAVE SOME REAL FUN!
THUMP
TMP TMP
HOLD IT!!
TMP

FWOOM
!?
GHOOOOO
SHULOOM
IT... WENT... INSIDE ME.
THAT WAS AMAZING! SYAORAN-KUN, DID THAT COME FROM YOU?
THAT'S A "KUDAN," HUH?
I'M NOT SURE. BUT I SUDDENLY GOT VERY HOT...

あ! OH!
YOU'RE OKAY, RIGHT?
NOD NOD
AND YOU, YOU'RE OKAY, TOO?
I'M GLAD FOR THAT!
BOW
HOOSH
EHH?!
HE VANISHED!
OH!
ぽん
PAPH
THAT KID WAS A KUDAN!
THESE KUDAN ...
IT LOOKS LIKE THEY CAN BE ANYTHING!

NOW, WHERE CAN MY "ALMOST KUDAN" HAVE GOTTEN OFF TO?
ん? HMM?
きょろ GLANCE
GASP
MOKONA!!
AAAH!
IT PROBABLY GOT STEPPED ON SOMEWHERE AROUND HERE.
LIKE SOME DISCARDED PORK BUN.
めんどくせー WHAT A PAIN!
ぽりぽり SKRITCH SKRITCH
いやー NOOOO.
ほら LOOK.
THE TRUTH IS QUITE DIFFERENT.
IT'S SO CUTE!
きゃ KYAA!
きゃ KYAA!
きゃ KYAA!
LOOK HOW SOFT!
THE SWEET-EST THING!
MOKONA IS POPULAR WITH THE LADIES!

BYE-BYE!
バイバーイ
KYAA!
KYAA!
BYE-BYE!
バイバーイ
MOKONA, WHERE WERE YOU?
ON TOP OF KUROGANE.
BUT THEN, MOKONA FELL OFF!
BUT JUST EARLIER . . .
. . . MOKONA WENT . . .
聞ーて!
LISTEN!
聞ーて!
LISTEN!
. . . JUST LIKE THIS!!
めきょ
BOINK
BUT NOBODY PAID ANY ATTENTION!
YOU MEAN THAT SAKURA'S FEATHER IS SOMEWHERE NEARBY?

DID YOU FIGURE OUT WHO HAD IT?
IT WAS...
BUT MOKONA DOESN'T FEEL IT ANYMORE.
ふるる
SHAKE SHAKE SHAKE
DON'T KNOW.
OH... I SEE.
しょんぼり
GLOOM
うーん
HMM.
EVEN IF WE LIMIT IT TO THE PEOPLE WHO WERE HERE, IT'LL STILL BE A LONG SEARCH.
THERE WERE LOTS OF PEOPLE.
STILL, WE NOW KNOW THAT SOMEONE CLOSE BY HAS IT.
THAT'S PRETTY GOOD PROG-RESS.
AND IF YOU SENSE ANYTHING MORE, LET US KNOW.
YES!
MOKONA WILL GO ALL-OUT!
THUMP

BUT IF KURO-CHI NEVER DROPPED MOKONA, THIS WOULDN'T HAVE HAPPENED.
WHAT MAKES THIS MY FAULT! AND WILL YOU STOP CALLING ME THOSE NAMES?!
BOW
I JUST WANTED TO THANK YOU!
MY NAME IS MASAYOSHI SAITÔ.
PLEASE LET ME DO SOMETHING FOR YOU IN THANKS!
NO, WE REALLY DIDN'T DO ANYTHING . . .
BUT . . . BUT . . .
MOKONA WANTS LUNCH!!
SOMETHING REALLY GOOD!
はーい
HEEEERE!
GUIDE US THERE.
教えて!
EH?
OKAY!
はいっ

32番街
営業中
SSSZZZZ
WHAT IS...
STARE
B-BMP
B-BMP
あの あの
UMM... UMM...
Y'SEE... OKONOMIYAKI IS *MY* FAVORITE DISH, SO...
I ORDERED MODAN-YAKI, BUT MAYBE TONPEI-YAKI WOULD HAVE BEEN BETTER.
"OKONOMIYAKI"? IS THAT WHAT THIS IS CALLED?
えっ?
EH?
OKONOMIYAKI IS A STAPLE OF THE DIET IN THE HANSHIN REPUBLIC.
IF YOU DON'T KNOW, THEN THAT MUST MEAN...

あ
AH!
...YOU COME FROM OUTSIDE THE COUNTRY?
YOU'VE GOT BLOND HAIR, TOO.
STARE
"OUTSIDE"? YOU COULD SAY THAT.
??
DO THOSE PEOPLE ALWAYS RUN ROUGHSHOD AROUND THIS DISTRICT?
THE GUYS WITH THE CAPS AND THE ONES IN THE GOGGLES?
THAT WAS...
...A FIGHT FOR DOMINANCE.
THEY FORM INTO TEAMS AND FIGHT TO SEE WHOSE KUDAN IS THE STRONGER.
AND...
...THE STRONGEST CLAIMS THE RIGHTS TO THE TERRITORY?

BUT THINK OF THE LIVES PUT IN DANGER WHEN THEY FIGHT IN SUCH A LARGE PUBLIC PLACE.
THAT'S TRUE, HUH?
MASAYOSHI-KUN HERE WAS IN BIG TROUBLE.
THIS OKONOMIYAKI LOOKS GREAT!
THAT'S BECAUSE I'M JUST USELESS.
THERE . . .
. . . THERE ARE BAD TEAMS, BUT THERE ARE GOOD TEAMS, TOO!
THEY PATROL THEIR TERRITORY MAKING SURE NO BAD KIDS CAUSE TROUBLE.
AND IF BAD PEOPLE ARE AROUND, THEY TAKE CARE OF THE PROBLEM!
LIKE A LOCAL MILITIA?
WHAT ABOUT THOSE TWO TEAMS BEFORE?
STARE
THE ONES IN CAPS WERE THE BAD ONES!
BUT THE ONES IN GOGGLES AREN'T LIKE THEM AT ALL!
WHEN THEY BATTLE OTHER TEAMS, SOME OF THE SURROUNDING BUILDINGS GET DAMAGED, SO THE ADULTS ARE AFRAID OF THEM . . . BUT THEY WOULDN'T DO ANYTHING ELSE THAT'S BAD!
THEY'RE REALLY COOL!

ESPECIALLY THEIR LEADER, SHÔGO-SAN!
THEY SAY HIS KUDAN IS SPECIAL LEVEL!
IT'S SO BIG AND STRONG... EVERYONE WISHES THEY HAD A KUDAN JUST LIKE IT!
OH!
SMELLS GREAT!
STARE
ZLIP ZLIP
S-L-U-M-P
BLUSH
STARE
I...
I'M SORRY.
THUMPA
THUMPA
THUMPA
STARE
AND YOU WISH YOU HAD A FRIEND JUST LIKE HIM, HUH?
I-I SURE DO!
LOOK AT ALL THE CABBAGE!
STAAAAARE

BUT I'D ALSO LIKE A FRIEND LIKE SYAORAN-KUN!
EH?
ANYBODY WITH A SPECIAL LEVEL KUDAN ...
鶴橋 風月
...IS JUST AMAZING!
じー
STARE
DIDN'T THE LEADER OF THAT GOGGLE TEAM SAY SOMETHING ABOUT A SPECIAL KUDAN...?
HMM.
SO, WHAT IS THAT? SPECIAL LEVEL?
IT'S AN ESPECIALLY HIGH LEVEL FOR KUDAN.

THE FOURTH-LEVEL KUDAN IS THE LOWEST.
AND MOVING UP, THERE'S THE THIRD LEVEL, SECOND LEVEL, FIRST LEVEL ...
... AND AT THE VERY TOP IS THE SPECIAL LEVEL.
特級
一級
二級
三級
四級
YEARS AGO, ALL THE COUNTRIES GOT TOGETHER AND BANNED THE USE OF LEVELS ON KUDAN ...
... BUT NORMAL PEOPLE STILL USE THE SYSTEM.
TWTCH
THEN ...
... THAT LEADER'S KUDAN MUST BE VERY STRONG.
YEAH!

SO IS SYAORAN-KUN'S!
TO GET A STRONG KUDAN, ESPECIALLY A SPECIAL-LEVEL KUDAN, YOU NEED TO BE A STRONG PERSON YOURSELF, OR THEY WON'T STAY!
IT'S A PERSON'S HEART THAT CONTROLS A KUDAN.
SO IF A PERSON CAN COMMAND A STRONG KUDAN, THAT'S PROOF THAT THE PERSON IS STRONG!
WHO WOULDN'T WANT A FRIEND LIKE THAT?
MY KUDAN . . .
. . . IS FOURTH LEVEL— THE VERY BOTTOM.
KLNCH
MASAYOSHI-KUN . . .

BUT WHEN DID SYAORAN-KUN'S KUDAN JOIN UP WITH HIM?
TWTCH
TWTCH
TWTCH
HMM?
NOW THAT YOU MENTION IT . . .
HM?
A DREAM?
SWIPP
I HAD AN ODD DREAM LAST NIGHT.
STOP RIGHT THERE !!
SWATT
POIT
EYAAH!
GMM

DOOOM
KINOMOTO
YUKITO
YOUR MAJESTY!
AND THE HIGH PRIEST!

Chapitre.7
Linked Worlds

ツバサ

RESERVoir CHRoNiCLE

えっ? EH?
えっ? EH?
Y— YOUR MAJESTY, WHAT BRINGS YOU HERE?
はぁ? HENH?
YOU GOT THE WRONG GUY.
"YOUR MAJESTY" IS NOWHERE IN MY NAME.
WHAT?
AND MISTER . . .
. . . WE DO THE FLIPPING HERE.
IF YOU'D JUST LEAVE IT AND WAIT, WE'LL BE RIGHT THERE.
Y— YES, SIR!

"YOUR MAJESTY"! THAT SOUNDS COOL!
LEAVE IT, WILL YA?
MAJESTY... WAS HE A KING IN YOUR WORLD?
YES...
AND THE GUY WITH HIM WAS THE HIGH PRIEST...
WITH OKONOMIYAKI HERE, THE WAITERS DO ALL THE COOKING FOR YOU.
YOU DON'T HAVE TO DO ANYTHING.
IS THAT RIGHT...?
BUSTLE
てきぱき
IT'S JUST LIKE THE SPACE-TIME WITCH SAID...
うるせー
SHADDUP!
しかられた
YOU GOT YELLED AT!
"PEOPLE YOU'VE MET ON YOUR WORLD..."
"...THEY'VE DEVELOPED UNDER COMPLETELY DIF-FERENT CONDITIONS ON OTHER WORLDS."

THEY'RE THE SAME... AND NOT THE SAME.
THE TWO FROM SYAORAN'S WORLD LIVED A COMPLETELY DIFFERENT LIFE THAN THESE TWO.
EXCUSE ME?
YOU'RE SAYING THAT THEY'RE THE SAME AS THE KING AND HIGH PRIEST OF THE KID'S WORLD?
BUT WHEN IT COMES DOWN TO IT...
...AT THE VERY BASIC LEVEL, THEY'RE THE SAME.
I GUESS.
BASIC LEVEL?
THE VERY ROOT OF THEIR LIVES.
THEIR NATURE... THEIR HEARTS...
"SOUL"!
THAT'S WHAT YOU'RE SAYING, RIGHT?

FROM NOW ON, I'M CALLING YOU, "YOUR MAJESTY."
DON'T YOU DARE!
I WONDER IF HIS MAJESTY AND THE HIGH PRIEST ARE ALL RIGHT.
DID THE COUNTRY CARRY ON ALL RIGHT AFTER THE FIGHT?
YES.
THOSE TWO WOULD MAKE SURE EVERY-THING'S FINE.

AND I MUST DO EVERYTHING POSSIBLE...
...TO RETURN THE FEATHERS OF SAKURA'S MEMORY!
...TO SAVE THE LIFE OF THE PRINCESS!

SYAORAN-KUN?
HUH?
IF YOU DON'T EAT IT, WE WILL.
OKAY!
THESE "CHOP-STICKS" ARE HARD TO USE!
AH! あの…
WE CAN ORDER ANOTHER!
DOWN THE HATCH!
いただきます!
LISTEN YOU!
THIS ONE'S MINE!!
GRATCH
TUGG TUGG TUGG
THAT WAS...
...GREAT!!
風月
ぷはー
MMPAAAAAHH
IT REALLY WAS.
GOOD JOB GUIDING US HERE.
IT REALLY *DID* TASTE GOOD!
OPEN
GLARE
IF YOU KNOW ANY OTHER GOOD PLACES, TELL US!
"TAKO-YAKI," FRIED OCTOPUS, IS REALLY GOOD, TOO!

NOW . . .
WHAT'S THE PLAN FROM HERE?
I THOUGHT WE WOULD SEARCH IN THIS SECTION OF TOWN.
ARE YOU GUYS GOING SOME-WHERE?
YES.
WHERE WOULD THAT BE?
WE DON'T REALLY KNOW. WE'RE SEARCH-ING FOR SOME-THING.
HM.
BUT WE DON'T KNOW OUR WAY AROUND, SO WE WON'T BE ABLE TO GO FAR.
WE HAVE TO BE ABLE TO FIND OUR WAY BACK TO SORA CHAN'S APARTMENT.
UH . . . EXCUSE ME.
IF IT'S OKAY WITH YOU, I'LL HELP YOU LOOK.
I CAN SHOW YOU AROUND.
WE DON'T WANT TO PUT YOU OUT . . .
NOT AT ALL!
BUT I SHOULD PHONE HOME FIRST.
IF YOU'D JUST WAIT HERE A SECOND . . .
TMP

MOKONA WILL MAKE A PHONE CALL, TOO!
HELLO? HELLO? HELLO?
TMP TMP TMP
HE REALLY DOES WANT TO BE FRIENDS, HUH?
STARE
I NEARLY FORGOT.
OUR CONVER-SATION WAS CUT OFF.
YOU WERE TALKING ABOUT YOUR DREAM ...
YES ...
IT WAS ABOUT THAT CREATURE THAT APPEARED ...
...THAT BEAST OF FIRE.
IF YOU'RE TALKING ABOUT DREAMS OF WEIRD ANIMALS... I HAD ONE, TOO.
ME, AS WELL.
IT WAS VERY PERSISTENT.
STAMP
I WANNA KNOW WHO THIS "SYAORAN" IS.

YOU HAVE BUSINESS WITH HIM?
ARE YOU THE ONE WHO SHÔGO SAID HE "LIKES YOUR STYLE"?
DOOM
へにゃっ
HEH HENH
AND WHAT IF I AM?
......

I'M SYAORAN.
ARE YOU SERIOUS?
A LITTLE KID?
NO, HE'S THE GUY! I'M SURE OF IT!
AND YOUR PLAN IS TO JOIN SHÔGO'S TEAM?
TEAM?
SHÔGO ALREADY HAS TOO MANY TOP-LEVEL PEOPLE ON HIS TEAM!
ANY MORE WILL TIP THE BALANCE!
EVEN SHÔGO ADMITTED THAT YOU HAVE A REALLY STRONG KUDAN!

IF YOU INTEND TO JOIN SHÔGO'S TEAM, I'M GONNA HAVE TO STOP YOU!
ZWIP
I'M NOT JOINING.
I'M NOT JOINING YOU EITHER.
きぱっ
NOT A CHANCE!
LOOKIN' GOOD, SYAORAN!
HE DOESN'T MINCE WORDS, DOES HE?
THEN YOU'LL JOIN *MY* TEAM!
お! YEAH!
YEAH!
YEAH!
YEAH!
I HAVE MY OWN AFFAIRS.
SO…
GRR
THEN YOU'RE PLANNING TO START A TEAM OF *YOUR OWN!!*
GRRAAAHH!
WHA-?
NO, YOU'RE NOT GET-TING—
FWAA

WELL, I'M GONNA TAKE YOU OUT RIGHT NOW!!
WOOOOOOOW
THAT'S HUGE!

DWOOOM
I'M NOT DOING ANY SUCH THING!
GWOOOM
BAM

ZEEEEEEEN
YAAAH!
YAAAH!
TMP TMP
YAAAH!
TMP
YAAAH!
TMP
YAAAH!
SSST
HM?
ん?
HM?
ん?
NOT A GOOD LISTENER, IS HE?
TUMP
I'VE BEEN PRETTY BORED HERE.
KRAKL

DOOM
I'LL TAKE YOU ON!
KURO-GANE'S BEEN LOOKING FORWARD TO THIS!
HE WASN'T BORED AT ALL!
THE HANSHIN REPUBLIC IS JUST HIS STYLE, HUH?
SHUT UP, OVER THERE!
ZAPH
BUT...
...KUROGANE-SAN!
YOU GAVE YOUR SWORD TO THAT WOMAN...

THAT SWORD WAS MAGIC.
IT WAS SPECIAL.
AND IN *MY* JAPAN, I NEEDED IT TO KILL THE MONSTERS THAT LIVED THERE.
BUT KUDAN ...
...AREN'T MONSTERS.
SO... WHAT LEVEL IS *YOUR* KUDAN?
HEH
I DON'T KNOW, AND I DON'T CARE.
WHAT'S ALL THE *TALK* FOR?
COME AND GET ME!

SYAORAN-KUN!!
YAAAHH
YAAAHH
YAAAHH
YAAAHH
MASAYOSHI-KUN, DO YOU KNOW THIS GUY?
IT'S A TEAM THAT WANTS TO CONTROL THIS DISTRICT!
THEY'RE BATTLING SHÔGO'S TEAM OVER IT!
IS THEIR LEADER ANY GOOD?
HIS KUDAN IS *FIRST LEVEL!*
HE MAY NOT LOOK LIKE MUCH, BUT HIS KUDAN IS ONE OF THE FASTEST AROUND!
AND...
TAKE A LOOK AT THE ATTACK OF A FIRST-LEVEL KUDAN!
EAT THIS!!

KANI-NABE SENKAI!*
VWAAAM
POK
*CRAB-POT REVOLUTION
PAKOW
IT SLICED RIGHT THROUGH!
ZUU
SKRRRRT
THAT KUDAN CAN SHARPEN PARTS OF ITS BODY TO AN EDGE AS SHARP AS A KNIFE!

POK
VWAARAAMM
TMP
TMP
TMP
TMP
GO!!
GO!!
TMP
SLA KOW
WATCH OUT!!
I THINK IF YOU TRY TO GET INVOLVED, HE'LL GET REALLY MAD.
KURO-TAN'S LIKE THAT.

JAA KIIIIIN
KANI DÔRAKU !!*
*CRAB FREE-STYLE
KUROGANE SAN!!
WHERE'S YOUR KUDAN?
YOU'RE PROBABLY SO WEAK, YOU'RE ASHAMED TO BRING IT OUT!
AHHHHH
HA
HA
HA
KRMBLE KRMBLE

OH, SHUT UP!
KRMBL
YOU GUYS TALK TOO MUCH!
MY KUDAN HAS AN EVEN TOUGHER SHELL THAN MOST FIRST-LEVEL KUDAN!
NICE, BOSS-MAN!
BUT IT HAS A WEAK-NESS.
あ
AWW...
IF I HAD A SWORD, IT'D BE IN PIECES ALREADY.

SHWAAA
!!

SHWAAA
WHAT?!
YOU WERE THE ONE THAT APPEARED IN MY DREAM!

SHWAAAA AAA
SHINGG
YOU'RE ASKING ME TO WIELD YOU?
I GET IT.
YOU LIKE A GOOD PUNCH-UP, TOO!

S-SO THAT'S YOUR KUDAN? IT'S PROBABLY ALL SHOW!
WELL, I'VE GOT AN ULTIMATE ATTACK!
KANE KUI-HÔDAI !!*
VWO OOM
IT DOESN'T MATTER HOW HARD A SHELL IS, WHEN YOU PULL OUT A KNIFE...
LOBSTERS AND CRABS ALL HAVE WEAK POINTS IN THE JOINTS.
*ALL-YOU-CAN-EAT CRAB

*MAGIC WAVE: DRAGON KING SWORD

DOOOOM

GAAAAAAAAAAAAAA!!

ARE YOU OKAY, BOSS?
HANG IN THERE!
MY KUDAN!
MY KUDAAAAN!!
YAAAH!!
YAAAH!!
YAAAH!!
TH-THE KID LIED!
HE *DID* FORM A TEAM!
WHEEZE
WHEEZE
YOU'RE A PART OF SYAORAN'S TEAM, AREN'T YOU?
I'M NOT ON *ANY-BODY'S* TEAM!
LISTEN...
...IN MY LIFE, I'VE ONLY SERVED UNDER ONE PERSON!

AND THAT'S PRINCESS TOMOYO!

Chapitre.8
The Country Where Gods Live

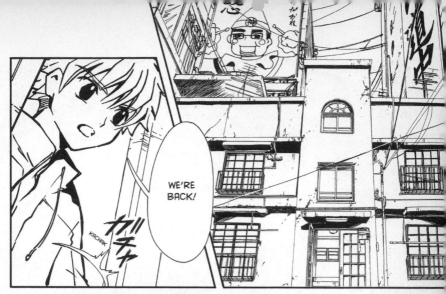

WE'RE BACK!
KACHAK
WE'RE BACK!
WE'RE BACK!
SST
WELCOME.
COME ON IN.
WERE YOU ABLE TO FIND ANY CLUES?
TMP
TMP
TMP
YES!
OH!
YOU'RE ALL HERE!
HOW'D IT GO?

BUT . . .
. . . BEFORE ANY OF THAT . . .
HONEY !!
MMMMMM!
WHERE'S MY "WELCOME HOME" KISS?! ♥
PUT IT HERE, BABE!
I SEE . . .
YOU HAD A REACTION, BUT IT DISAPPEARED.

AND...
THROB じんじん THROB
...JUST WHEN SYAORAN WAS IN TROUBLE, SOMETHING THAT LOOKED LIKE A BEAST OF FIRE SUDDENLY APPEARED.
WHAT A HUGE BUMP!
ARASHI'S REALLY STRONG
AHIRU
THAT'S RIGHT.
THAT BEAST MUST HAVE BEEN YOUR KUDAN, SYAORAN-KUN.
BOING ぴょん
WELL...
IT SEEMS LIKE A PRETTY STRONG ONE, TOO!
AND KUROGANE'S KUDAN ALSO SEEMS STRONG!
HOW DO YOU KNOW THAT?

I TOLD YOU BEFORE . . .
. . . I'M A SCHOLAR OF HISTORY.
THE KUDAN ARE THE LINCHPIN OF THE WHOLE THING.
IT'S MY BELIEF . . .
. . . THAT KUDAN ARE AKIN TO GODS IN THIS NATION.
IN THE HANSHIN REPUBLIC, THERE IS A MYTH THAT'S BEEN HANDED DOWN THROUGH THE AGES . . .
IT SAYS THAT THE NUMBER OF KAMI, GODS, IS "YAOYOROZU."
HANSIN
八百万
"YAOYOROZU"?
IT'S SPELLED WITH THE CHARACTERS FOR "EIGHT MILLION."
SO THERE ARE EIGHT MILLION GODS HERE?
LOTS OF...
...KAMI-SAMA!
NO, PROBABLY MANY MORE.
THEY SAY THERE ARE AS MANY GODS AS THERE ARE THINGS AND PHENOMENA IN THE WORLD.
THE WORD "YAOYOROZU" REALLY SIMPLY MEANS, "A WHOLE LOT."

SO THE GODS OF THAT MYTH ARE NOW CALLED KUDAN?
THAT'S PRETTY IMPRESSIVE.
YOU LIVE TOGETHER WITH YOUR GODS.
SO THE GODS OF THIS LAND ...
...PROTECT EACH AND EVERY PERSON WHO LIVES IN IT!
WHOOSH
YOU CAME TO THAT CONCLUSION, TOO?
I'VE THOUGHT THAT ALL ALONG!
THE KUDAN, OR RATHER THE GODS, HAVE A LASTING LOVE FOR THE PEOPLE OF THIS COUNTRY!

EVERY PERSON, WITHOUT EXCEPTION, IS ACCOMPANIED BY A KUDAN.
SO EVERY HUMAN IN THIS COUNTRY IS PROTECTED!
NOT ONE IS LEFT ALONE!
IT'S TRUE . . .
. . . THAT A LOT OF PEOPLE IN THE HANSHIN REPUBLIC ARE EASY TO GET RILED UP.
THEY HATE LOSING; THEY NEVER GET TO THE POINT; THEY'LL ATTACK IF YOU'RE NOT PAYING ATTENTION; IF OUR TEAM WINS THEY GO CRAZY; THEY THROW THEMSELVES IN THE RIVER . . .
BUT EVEN SO . . .
. . . I THINK THEY REALLY ARE GOOD PEOPLE.
AND THAT'S WHY . . .
. . . WHEN IT COMES TO FINDING SAKURA'S FEATHER . . .
. . . SEARCHING HERE IS PROBABLY BETTER THAN SEARCHING IN A COUNTRY FULL OF BAD PEOPLE, OR A COUNTRY THAT MAKES WAR ON ITS NEIGHBORS.
.....
YES.

YOU SAID THAT YOU DETECTED THE WAVES OF SAKURA'S FEATHER, BUT YOU DON'T KNOW WHERE IT WENT?
しょぼん…
SLUMP
UH-HUH.
SO IF IT WERE SIMPLY SOMEONE WHO HAD THE FEATHER AND WALKED AWAY...
...YOU PROBABLY COULD HAVE EASILY TRACKED DOWN WHERE IT WENT TO.
BUT IF THE ONE THAT HAD IT COULD APPEAR AND DISAPPEAR...
...THE ONLY THING THAT COULD HAVE IT IS...
AHIRU

GASP
A KUDAN!
IS THAT WHAT YOU MEAN?
なるほど
MAKES SENSE.
A KUDAN *CAN* APPEAR AND DISAPPEAR.
AND IF A KUDAN DISAPPEARED, THE WAVE MIGHT DIS-APPEAR, TOO.
WITHIN ONE OF THESE KUDAN...
...WE MAY FIND SAKURA'S FEATHER!
BUT WE HAVE NO IDEA JUST WHO HAD THE KUDAN WITH THE FEATHER.
IT WAS IN THE MIDDLE OF A TERRITORIAL BATTLE.
THERE WERE WHOLE LOTS OF KUDAN BACK THERE!

BUT...
...IT WOULD HAVE TO BE A STRONG KUDAN.
WHY DO YOU SAY THAT?
AHIRU
THE FRAGMENTS OF SAKURA'S MEMORY...
...ARE IMMENSELY POTENT—LIKE CRYSTALLIZED SHARDS OF HER HEART.
A KUDAN USES THE OWNER'S HEART.
THE STRONGER THE HEART, THE STRONGER THE KUDAN BECOMES.
IN ANY CASE ...
...LOOKING FOR THE STRONGEST KUDAN SEEMS LIKE A SHORTCUT TO FINDING SAKURA'S FEATHER.
NOD
MOKONA WILL SEARCH REAL HARD!

よし!
ALL RIGHT!
SINCE WE'VE GOT THAT ALL DECIDED, IT'S TIME TO FORTIFY OURSELVES WITH SOME GOOD FOOD!
TODAY WE HAVE BEEF UDON NOODLES AND FRIED TOFU SUSHI.
I MADE ALL THE ARRANGEMENTS BEFORE GOING OFF TO WORK.
FSSH
FSSH
I WILL NEED THE HELP OF KUROGANE AND FAI.
WHY DO I HAVE TO HELP?
IF YOU DON'T WORK, YOU DON'T EAT.
MOKONA'S GOING TO EAT, SO MOKONA WILL WORK!
I'LL HELP TOO.
NOT TODAY, YOU DON'T.
YOU WERE AWAY FROM SAKURA ALL DAY.
YOU WERE WORRIED, WEREN'T YOU?
YOU CAN STAY AND WATCH HER.
WHEN DINNER IS READY, I'LL GIVE YOU A CALL.
KREEE
THANKS!
THANKS A LOT!
KACHAK

YOUR HIGHNESS, ARE YOU ALL RIGHT?
I *TOLD* YOU TO QUIT THE "POLITE" TALK!
HMPH!
HMPH!
PLEASE FORGIVE ME—
NO . . .
I MEAN . . .
SORRY.
BUT, REALLY, ARE YOU OKAY?
EH
HEH
HEH
I'M FINE.
IT'S JUST A LITTLE FEVER.
EVEN THE DOCTOR SAID THAT IT'LL GO DOWN WITH JUST A BIT OF REST.
OH!
BUT WAIT…

THEY ALSO SAY THAT IF SOME-ONE HOLDS YOUR HAND ...
...YOU GET BETTER FASTER.
TOO MUCH TO ASK?
GRP
UMM...
YOU REALLY SHOULD GET SOME SLEEP.
YOU'LL STAY HERE WITH ME?
YEAH.

IF I FALL ASLEEP LIKE THIS...
...THE FIRST THING I'LL SEE WHEN I WAKE UP...
...WILL BE YOU, SYAORAN.

I'LL DO ANYTHING TO WAKE SAKURA AS QUICKLY AS I CAN!
I'LL FIND HER FEATHERS!
I WILL!

I GUESS THAT NOBODY HAS THEIR KUDAN OUT WHILE SIMPLY WALKING.
AND IF THEY DON'T, WE'LL NEVER SEE IF ANYONE'S KUDAN IS STRONGER OR WEAKER.
ラーメン
HANS
EVEN IF...
EVEN IF...
...WE DO FIND OUT WHICH KUDAN HAS TAKEN THE FEATHER...
...I DOUBT THEY'LL BE OVERLY WILLING TO GIVE IT UP.
GWAAAM
AAH !!
ぺこり
BOW

TMP
TMP
TMP
TMP
SYAORAN-KUN!!
MASA-YOSHI-KUN.
HUFF
HUFF
WHEEZE
WHEEZE
WHOOSH
WERE YOU ABLE TO FIND WHAT YOU WERE LOOKING FOR AFTER I LEFT?
NOT YET...
OKAY, THEN HOW ABOUT I BE YOUR GUIDE AGAIN TODAY?
ARE YOU SURE IT'S OKAY?
BOING
SURE!
TODAY'S SUNDAY!
IT'S PERFECTLY FINE FOR TODAY!
I'M SURPRISED YOU WERE ABLE TO FIND US.
MY KUDAN CAN FIND ANYBODY AS LONG AS HE'S MET THEM ONCE.
IT'S NO GOOD IF IT'S TOO FAR AWAY, THOUGH.
THAT'S PRETTY AMAZING!
AMAZING!
AMAZING!
BUT THAT'S ABOUT *ALL* HE CAN DO.
HE'S PRETTY WEAK!

JEEEEEEEEEN
!

GWOOON
KYAAH!
AAAAAH!!

JEEEEEN
MOKONA!
MASAYOSHI-KUN!!
FLIP
GASP
阪神城で待つ
I'll be waiting at Hanshin Castle!
DO
OOM

Chapitre.9
The Magician's Kudan

WHOOSH
FAI-SAN!
KUROGANE-SAN!
LOOK AT THIS!
!?
THIS PAPER CAME DOWN FROM THAT BIRD!
阪神城で待つ
I'll be waiting at Hanshin Castle!
THEY COULD HAVE TAKEN MOKONA AND MASAYOSHI-KUN TO THIS CASTLE!

CHATTER
CHATTER
CHATTER
CHATTER
CHATTER
今◎△×鳥■◎何飛◆◎連××?
КЦФ!!ЖЭф$Ы Ю□Чю́ЭЪП<У
HUH?

DONK DONK
とんとん
ЩЬКФб!?
#щЪ@ЛЖ
SKWEEK
ほじ
SKWEEK
ほじ
阪神城■◎
行××▲!?
NO, IT'S NOT THAT MY EARS HAVE GONE STRANGE.
Д8Чю
SWEAT
あわ
SWEAT
あわ
違◎!
BUT FOR SOME REASON, I DON'T UNDER-STAND THE WORDS!
AND IT'S NOT AS IF WE WENT ANYWHERE!
?
AAAH!!

MOKONA!!
MEE EEE!

ぷらーん
BURUUUUM
きゃっ
KYAA!
きゃっ
KYAA!
うわーん
WAAAAAH!!
UMM ... ARE YOU *SURE* THIS KID IS THE ONE?
THIS IS THE GUY SHÔGO SAID HE LIKED?
ABSOLUTELY CERTAIN, MA'AM!
HE WAS WITH THE SPIKY-HAIRED BIG GUY AND THE THIN BLOND GUY.
AND ...
...THE SMALLEST ONE IN THE GROUP IS "SYAORAN."
うす!!
ZOOOM
WE HAVE A WINNER!
HMMMM.

SUBWAY
HANSHIN CASTLE FRONT ENTRANCE STATION
HANSHIN CASTLE IS THIS WAY!
TMP TMP TMP TMP
ЖЪФЛ
ぽりぽり
SKRICH SKRICH
面倒◎▲!
HANSHIN MAP
I KNEW THEY WOULDN'T UNDER-STAND ME!
WHOOM

ぷらーん
BULUUUUN
MOKONA!
MASAYOSHI-KUN!
HOW'D YOU GET UP THERE!?
おーい
HEEEEY!
YOU LOOK LIKE YOU'RE HAVING *FUN!*
AT LEAST THE WHITE THING DOES!
あ
AH!
SO YOU UNDER-STAND ME NOW?
YEAH.
I GET IT NOW.
AT LEAST WHAT YOU TWO ARE SAYING.
SO IT *IS* MOKONA THAT'S DOING IT.

MOKONA WAS SERVING AS A TRANSLATION DEVICE.
SWING, SWING, I'M JUST LIKE A BALLOON!
BLOW, WIND, BLOW!
AND BLOW SOME MORE!
MOKONA IS PRETTY INCREDIBLE!
TRANSPORTING US TO OTHER WORLDS . . .
TRANSLATING OUR LANGUAGES FOR US . . .
EATING APPLES WHOLE . . .
HEY!
DOES THIS MEAN THAT ANY TIME WE GET SEPARATED FROM IT, WE WON'T BE ABLE TO COMMUNI-CATE?
THAT'S WHAT IT MEANS.
TMP
AWW!
TMP TMP
WHAT A PAIN!!
TMP TMP TMP TMP TMP

A LOT OF THEM, HUH?
WHAT'S WITH THESE PEOPLE?!
CHATTER
CHATTER
CHATTER
DOOOM
DOOOM
WHO IS THE ONE WHO WROTE THIS LETTER?!
THAT WOULD BE ME!! ♪
BOOOM
I'll be waiting at

うおお!
YEAAAAAAAAAH!
PRIMERA-CHAN!!
WHO IS THIS WOMAN?!
YOU DON'T KNOW PRIMERA-CHAN?!
YOU MUST LIVE UNDER A ROCK!!
BOO!
BOO!
BOO!
BOO!
PRIMERA-CHAN IS OUR IDOL!!
SHE SINGS! SHE DANCES! SHE MODELS! SHE EVEN HAS A MORNING TALK SHOW!
MORE THAN THAT, SHE CONTROLS AN INCREDIBLE KUDAN!
CUTE AND STRONG!
SHE'S THE BEST!!

PLEASE LET MOKONA AND MASAYOSHI-KUN DOWN!
WHOM
I AM SYAORAN!
BULUUUUN
YOU MEAN THAT ISN'T "SYAORAN"?
POIT
BAM BAM BAM BAM BAM
YOU IDIOTS!!
RAPID-FIRE HITS
YOU COULDN'T HAVE BEEN MORE WRONG!!
OWW!
UFF!
IF YOU HAVE ANY BUSINESS, BRING IT TO ME!
LET THOSE TWO DOWN RIGHT NOW, PLEASE!
TUMP
NOPE!

PRIMERA-CHAN!
YEAAAAAAAAH!
IF YOU WANT THEM BACK, YOU'RE GOING TO HAVE TO *BATTLE* ME FOR THEM!
PRIMERA-CHAN!
YEAAAH!
SHE'S SO CUTE!
PRIMERA-CHAN!!
LOVE
AWW!
SHAD-DAP!
SHE'S SO BEAUTIFUL!
WE'LL HAVE TO FIND A WAY UP!
I MIGHT BE ABLE TO GET UP THERE.
YOU KNOW WHERE THE STAIRCASE IS?
NO ...
BUT I SHOULD BE ABLE TO GET THERE.
YEAH? HOW?
MY KUDAN MAY BE WILLING TO HELP.

HOOWAAAAAAA

WAFFF
suuun

HWOO
HE'S FLYING!
THESE KUDAN COME IN *EVERY* TYPE.
HUMPH!
MAN!
HE CAN FLY?
NO FAIR!
IF I CAN'T, HE SHOULDN'T BE ALLOWED TO!

MY KUDAN, COME ON!!
SHUULULULU
SHUULULULU
NOW YOU'LL SEE WHAT KIND OF DAMAGE MY KUDAN'S ATTACK CAN DO!
CHINGG
HOO OOM

IS EVERYONE...
...HAVING FUN?! ♪
DMM

BZZT BZZT
IS EVERYONE HAVING FUN?!

DOHOOOM
FAI-SAN!!

Chapitre.10
Where the Feather Went

SWIP
LOOK UP THERE.
EH?
VWAM
THAT WAS A SURPRISE.
A KUDAN CAN DO THAT?
THIS COUNTRY IS PRETTY AMAZING.
YOU LIKED THAT ATTACK, DIDN'T YOU, MOKONA?
AMAZING!
AMAZING!
CLAP CLAP
WAAAAH!
PRIMERA-CHAN'S KUDAN IS SPECIAL LEVEL!
BE CAREFUL!

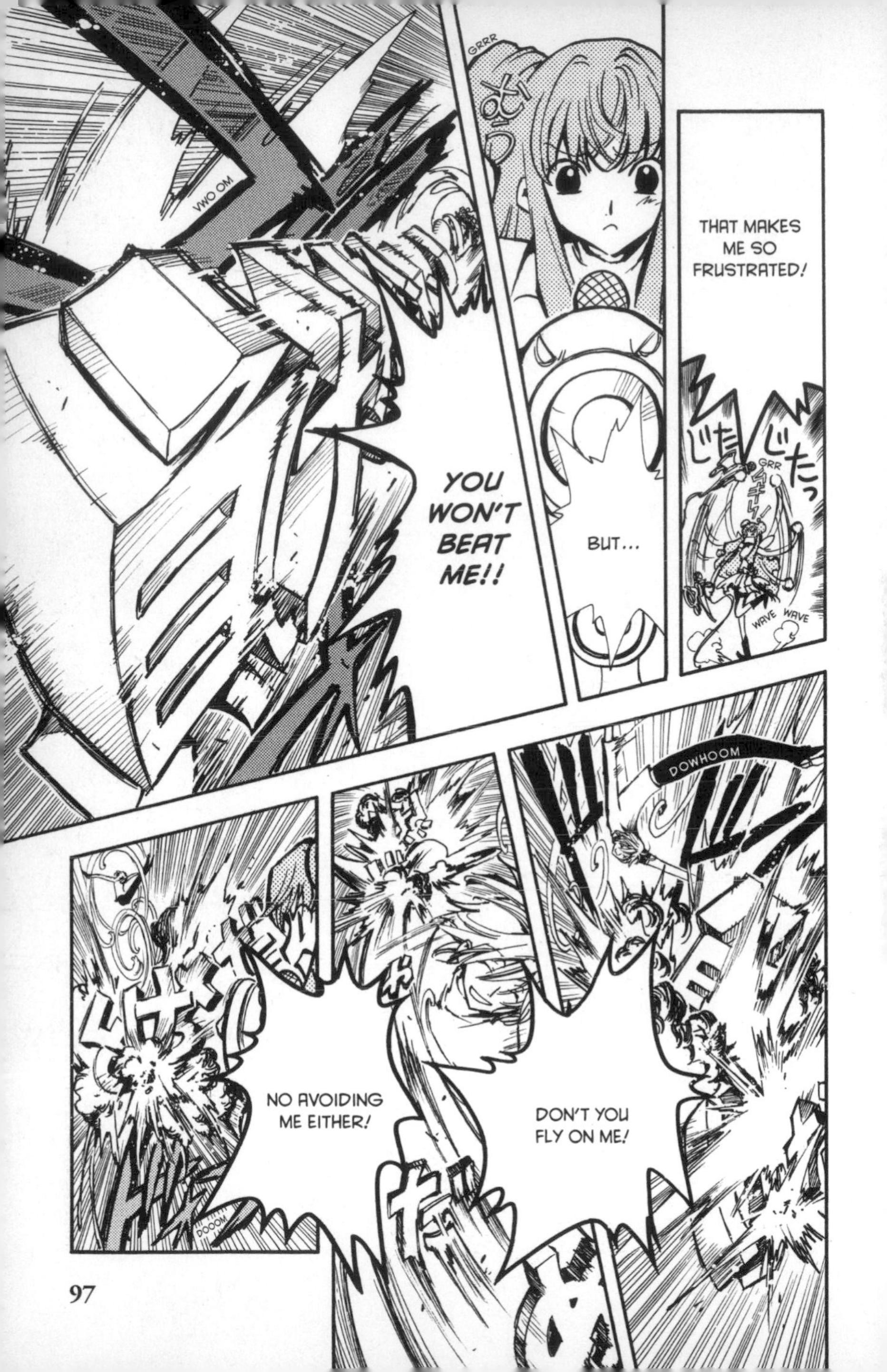
THAT MAKES ME SO FRUSTRATED!
GRR
WAVE WAVE
GRRR
BUT...
YOU WON'T BEAT ME!!
VWO OM
DOWHOOM
DON'T YOU FLY ON ME!
NO AVOIDING ME EITHER!
DOOOM

BOOOM
QUIT RUNNING AWAY!!
WAFT
WHY?
WHY CAN'T I *HIT* YOU?

IF I LET YOU HIT ME, IT MIGHT HURT.
HENH
GRR
YAAAH!
YAAAH!
GLANCE GLANCE
WHAT ARE YOU PLAN-NING?
YAAAH!
WE HAVE TO GET TO THE TOP AND GET THOSE TWO DOWN!
WE ALSO HAVE TO HELP FAI-SAN!
YOU CAN LEAVE *HIM* ALONE.
HE'LL BE FINE!
HMPH
BAAAM
A TUDOR WHO TOOTED A *FRUIT* TRIED TO TUTOR TWO *DOODOOS* TO TOOT!

KAM
miss
KAM
KAM
POK
THE SIXTH SHEIK'S *SICKO'S SHIP'S SUNK!*
miss
BAAM
I'VE FOUGHT WITH KUDAN, SO I KNOW.
EVEN IF YOUR KUDAN IS ABLE TO FLY, YOUR MUSCLES ARE YOUR BODY'S NORMAL MUSCLES.
PRIMERA-CHAN!!
EVEN HER MISTAKES ARE CUTE!
BBBOOM
YOU MEAN THE ABILITY TO FLOAT AND DODGE LIKE HE'S AS LIGHT AS PAPER... IS *FAI-SAN'S* OWN ABILITY?
POK
PAP
PAP
PAP
RED LORRY, YELLOW LORRY, RED LORRY, YELLOW *YORRY!*
A FLEA AND A FLY FLEW UP IN A FLUE, EE-AI-EE-AI-OH!
AH.

BBB BOOM
LOOK AT THAT DAMN GRIN!
THAT MAN IS A COMBAT VETERAN.
I IMAGINE SO.
BBOOM
EH ?!
YEAAAH!
YEAAAH!
THAT DOESN'T SURPRISE YOU?
THERE'S A CLUE IN THE CASUAL WAY FAI-SAN CARRIES HIMSELF...
...AND ...
...THE LOOK IN HIS EYES JUST GIVES YOU THAT IMPRESSION.
....

MAYBE YOU'RE *NOT* A COMPLETE FOOL.
BUT…I'D STILL LIKE TO HELP HIM OUT IF I CAN.
PRIMELA-CHAN!!
YEAAAH!
¡YEAAAH!
YEAAAH!
YEAAAH!
BUT…
I'M RIGHT ABOUT YOU BEING A NAIVE KID!
YOU FORCED ME INTO IT!
CHANGE!!
WOOOOOOW!!
LOVE
PRIMERA!
PRIMERA!

MY KUDAN, CHANGE FORM!!
ZLUUMMM
WHEN MY KUDAN-CHAN BECOMES A MIKE STAND...
...THERE'S NO RUNNING AWAY!
VWAMM
ZWEEEEEEEN
ALL THE FANS LOVE MEEEEEEE...

...EEEEEEEEEEEEEE...
ZWOOM
ZLIP
HEH!
...EE-
YEAH!

ZWOOOM

KAKK
FAI-
SAN!!
BBOOOM
SHUSH
FAI-
SAN!!
SHUSHH
I'M ALL
RIGHT!
SHAKK

I NEVER EXPECTED IT TO CHANGE FORM!
AND THOSE LETTERS SURE COME AFTER YOU!
PAT
PAT
AND SINCE THIS GIRL IS FIGHTING WITH HER KUDAN, AND MOKONA ISN'T REACTING...
...IT MUST MEAN THAT THE GIRL ISN'T THE ONE WITH THE FEATHER.
TWIRL, TWIRL.
I'M JUST LIKE A WATER BALLOON!
WHIRL, WHIRL.
SNIFF
SNIFF
AH HA HA!
WELL?
DO YOU SURRENDER?
YEAH!
YEAH!
IF I DID, WHAT WOULD HAPPEN NEXT?
THEN I MOVE ON TO THE NEXT ONE TO DEFEAT, THIS "SYAORAN" GUY!
WE CAN'T HAVE THAT.
SYAORAN-KUN HAS SOME IMPORTANT BUSINESS TO SEE THROUGH.

I'D REALLY RATHER THAT IT ENDS WITH ME.
YEAAH!
YEAAH!
YEAAH!
PRIMELA-CHAN!
PRIMELA-CHAN!
HEH
IF SO...
...THEN I...
WILL JUST HAVE TO WIIIIIIIIN!!
GWOOO
SWUP
THUMP

TMP
TMP
TMP
TMP
TMP
TMP
EH?!

I DON'T WANT TO BE THE CAUSE OF INJURY TO A BEAUTIFUL YOUNG WOMAN.
WON'T YOU STOP?
DAA

SNIFF
TH—
THIS IS SO NOT FAIR!!
B-
B-
BWOM
B-BOOM
AH!!
HYUUUUUU
WHEEE!
WAAAAAH!

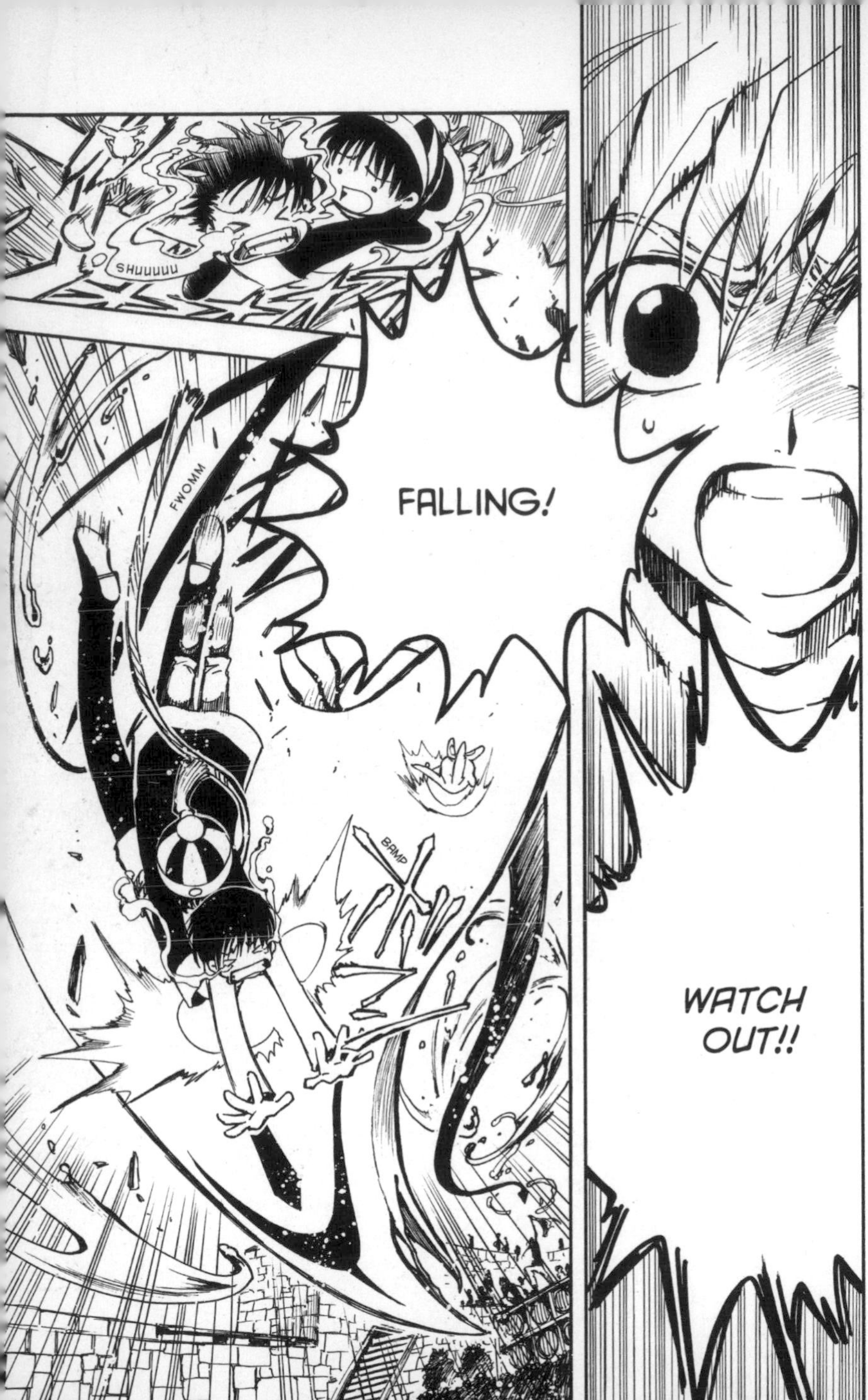
WATCH OUT!!
SHUUUUU
FALLING!
FWOMM
BAMP

WHAT DO YOU THINK YOU'RE *DOING*, PRIMERA?
SHÔGO-KUN!
BOINK

Chapitre.11
The Kudan of Fire

ツバサ
RESERVoir CHRoNiCLE

IT'S THAT LEADER FROM BEFORE!
YOU'VE GOT WORK TO DO, RIGHT?
HMPH!
YOU'RE AN IDOL, RIGHT?
DON'T YOU HAVE A CONCERT TO PREPARE FOR?
EVEN IF IT IS...
WHY ARE YOU DESTROYING OUR CULTURAL HERITAGE?!
DON'T BLAME ME IF THEY GET ALL MAD OVER IT!
BESIDES, THERE'S *PLENTY* OF TIME!
THE CONCERT'S AT THE HANSHIN DOME RIGHT OVER THERE!
I DID IT BECAUSE... BECAUSE *YOU* NEVER COME TO SEE ME!
YOU DON'T! YOU DON'T!
THANK YOU.

WHAT WAS THAT?!
なにィっ!!
YOU BREAK BUILDINGS ALL THE TIME, SHÔGO-KUN! DON'T TALK TO *ME* ALL HIGH AND MIGHTY!
WAFT
HUH?
あー?
WHAT ARE THESE TWO SQUABBLING ABOUT?
UH?
UH?
SNFFL
うっ
SNFFL
うっ
SNFFL
うっ
SNFFL
うっ
SNFFL
うっ
SNFFL
うっ
L O V E
HM?
WHAT ARE YOU ALL CRYING OVER?
WAAAAAH!
うわああん
PRIMERA-CHAN'S IN LOVE WITH THAT TEAM LEADER, THERE!
プリメーラちゃーん
PRIMERA-CHAN!
BUT ...
...SINCE HE NEVER COMES TO SEE HER, SHE'S LONELY!!
WAAAAAH!
うぉぉぉぉ

HOW DO YOU KNOW?
WHO WOULD YOU MOST LIKE TO BE WITH?
On Your Days Off
WAAAAAH!
PRIMERA-CHAN!!
SEE FOR YOURSELF!
PAK
VWOOSH
BECAUSE PRIMERA-CHAN MADE IT OFFICIAL!
VWOOSH
BUT SHE'S SOOO CUTE!!
STARE
YOU'RE LOOKING IN THE WRONG PLACE! LOOK AT THE PHOTO SPREAD IN FRONT!!
TORA WATER
WEEKLY 25
WAAAAAAH!!

I HEAR THAT THERE'S SOME TERRITORIAL RUMBLE GOING ON, SO I COME TO SEE WHAT'S UP, AND ...
FOOOM
I DON'T KNOW ABOUT YOU, BUT *I'M* SUPPOSED TO GO TO SCHOOL AND HELP OUT WITH THE FAMILY BUSINESS!
WE'RE RIGHT DOWN THE STREET!
YOU KNOW THE ADDRESS!
I WAS IN THE MIDDLE OF A DELIVERY!
ASAGI LIQUORS
浅黄酒店
WAAH!
BUT I'M *LONELY*!!
っていうか
THEY LOOK ...
YOU'RE SO DUMB!
違うし
... NOTHING ALIKE!
WAAAAAAAH!!
ぴょん
BOING
UM
SO I ASKED THIS GUY YOU LIKE OVER TO SEE ME, HOPING HE WOULD JOIN THE PRIMERA FAN CLUB, AND WHILE YOU VISITED WITH HIM, YOU COULD SEE *ME* TOO!

SYAORAN!
SYAORAN!
BOING
MOKONA!
YOUR *EYES!!*
ぴょん
BOING
ぴょん
BOING
IT'S HERE!
THE FEATHER IS *REAL* CLOSE BY!
ぴょん
ぴょん
BOING
BOING
WHERE?
WHO HAS IT?!
MOKONA DOESN'T KNOW!
BUT MOKONA JUST FELT A *HUGE* WAVE!

SO SOME KUDAN HAS TAKEN IT INSIDE ITSELF.
WHY ISN'T IT ONE FIXED STRENGTH?
BUT...
...IT GETS STRONGER AND THEN GETS WEAKER.
WHAT IS THAT SUPPOSED TO MEAN?
SORATA-SAN SAID THAT KUDAN PROTECT THEIR OWNERS.
SO PROBABLY, THE TIME THAT IT PUTS OUT ITS GREATEST STRENGTH IS WHEN IT'S PROTECTING ITS OWNER.
DOOOM
AND THAT MEANS...
...THE WAY TO FIND THE FEATHER IS THROUGH BATTLE!

I'M SORRY THAT MY WORDS CAUSED UN-EXPECTED TROUBLE FOR YOU…
… SYAORAN.
BUT I MEANT IT. I *DO* LIKE YOUR STYLE.
HEH
YOU'RE STRONG.
THUMP
AND BY THAT, I DON'T MEAN YOU GOT MUSCLES. RIGHT HERE.
SO I WANTED TO TRY TO TAKE YOU ON…
…WITH OUR KUDAN.
SHÔGO-KUN, ALL YOU CARE ABOUT ARE YOUR KUDAN BATTLES! YOU RETARD!
DON'T SAY "RETARD!"
CALL ME A "FOOL" OR AN "IDIOT" IF YOU LIKE.
I UNDER-STAND.
SST
PFF

THEN I ACCEPT...
...YOUR CHALLENGE!

SHHK
YOU GUYS, STAY OUTTA THIS, GOT ME?
FOWOOO!!
I BET 3000 KO ON SHŌGO!
I GOT MY MONEY ON SYRORAN!
2000 KO!!
LIKE I SAID IN MY DREAM, I WANT POWER.
POWER TO PROTECT SAKURA.
READY!
YOU'LL FIGHT ALONG-SIDE ME?
SSS
YEAAH!
YEAAH!
YEAAH!
SSHAA

GO!!
WHOOM

KRMBLE
KRMBLE
TMP
WATCH OUT!!
HOOM
WAA

WHEEET-WHOOO!
HE'S PRETTY COOL... ...SYAORAN-KUN.
SO HE'S MORE THAN JUST A PLIABLE FOOL.
YOU BOTH HAVE FACES THAT SAY, "IGNORE ME, I'M A FOOL!" BUT I SEE THROUGH IT.
YEAH.
IT SEEMS LIKE HE'S MORE THAN A GUY WITH AN ARCHAEOLOGY HOBBY.
HE'S STILL VERY YOUNG...
...BUT YOUNG PEOPLE CAN COME THROUGH THEIR PAIN.
AND I BELIEVE HE HAS.

MOKONA!
CAN YOU FEEL THE FEATHER'S WAVE?
THE WAVE *IS* THERE, BUT MOKONA DOESN'T KNOW WHO HAS IT!
NO NO NO
I GUESS WE WON'T KNOW UNTIL WE MAKE THE WAVE BIGGER.
I DON'T KNOW IF *THAT* KUDAN IS THE ONE WITH THE FEATHER...
...BUT THERE'S NO DOUBT THAT IT HAS TO BE A STRONG KUDAN!
SHHT
AND I HAVE TO MAKE SURE!!

SAKURA'S FEATHER IS CLOSE BY!!

GWOO

KAM
KAM
KAM
KAM
KAM
DOOOM
SHÔGO-
KUN!!

FWA SOOM
PLIP
PLIP
OH, MAN!
THAT WAS THE FIRST TIME I WAS EVER HIT LIKE THAT!
TUMP
SHÔGO-KUN!!
I'M FINE! I *TOLD* YOU TO STOP SCREAMING MY NAME!
YOU'LL RUIN YOUR VOICE JUST BEFORE A CONCERT!
WH— WHO EVER SAID I *CARED* WHAT HAPPENS TO YOU?!
WHSSH
WHSSH
DON'T TALK SO BIG! YOU'RE BREAKING STUFF TOO!
SHE'S SO CUTE!
CHATTER
CHATTER

REALLY!
YOU'RE A TOUGH ONE.
KUDAN ARE CONTROLLED BY THE HEART.
WHAT IS IT THAT MAKES YOURS SO STRONG?
I HAVE SOMETHING THAT I *MUST* SEE THROUGH.
THAT MAKES SENSE.

EVERYONE, GET OUTTA HERE!!
FAM
FOWOOO
SET!
GO!!
SHAAAAA
GWOOO

DOOOOOOOM
ZLUUU
KYAA!
KYAA!
GMMMMMMMMMM

SYAORAN-
KUN!!

SHAAAAAHH
THIS IS TERRIBLE!!
SYAORAN-KUN WILL GET WASHED AWAY!!
I HAVE TO FIND HIM!
WHERE?
WHERE?
SHUUU
SHHHH
HHHHH
EH?!
SYAORAN IS RIGHT THERE!

DOOM

...AMAZING...
へたん
SLUMP
HE SAID HE CAME FROM A FOREIGN COUNTRY...
BUT JUST LOOK AT THE WAY HE CONTROLS HIS KUDAN!
GRMP
ME TOO!
I WANT TO BE STRONG, TOO!

JUST LIKE HIM!
SHHHHHHHH
STRONG!
KNCH
KNCH

RMMBL
RMMBL
WATCH OUT!!
GAGARASSH
KYAAAAAH!!
NO!
I CAN'T LEAVE JUST TO SAVE MYSELF!
WHOO
NOT WHEN THERE ARE PEOPLE TO PROTECT!!

I HAVE
TO BE
STRONG
!!!
KAKK

zwuuuuuuuuuu

WHAAAAAP??
CLATTR
CLATTR
BOINK
MOKONA FOUND IT!
THE FEATHER!
IT'S IN THAT KUDAN!!

Chapitre.12
The Proof of Bravery

DID I HEAR RIGHT?
THE FEATHER'S IN THAT KUDAN?
IN *THAT* KUDAN?!
RMMMM
I THINK I SEE... EVEN WHEN HE USED HIS KUDAN TO FIND US, MOKONA DIDN'T DETECT IT.
BUT WHEN IT PROTECTS ITS MASTER...
THE TIME WHEN IT NEEDS THE MOST POWER IS WHEN IT IS PROTECTING SOMEONE IT CARES ABOUT FROM A LIFE-OR-DEATH SITUATION.

THE LAST TIME MOKONA DETECTED IT...
...WAS ALSO WHEN MASAYOSHI WAS IN A DANGEROUS SITUATION.
KRAKL
KRAKL
WAAAA!
YOU JUST PUT THAT BOY DOWN RIGHT NOW!
BATTA
BATTA
EVEN NOW, IT'S TRYING TO PROTECT HIM FROM THE CRUMBLING CASTLE.
SHOOOO
WOOOOO
SAKURA'S FEATHER...
...IS INSIDE THAT!

KYOOOOOO
KYAAAAAH!!
KRATTR
KRATTR
プリメーラちゃん!!
PRIMELA-CHAN!!

SHÔGO-KUN!
KASH
ZHOON
KRAKK
THERE, THERE.
PHEW!
WAAAAH!
I WAS SO SCARED !!
MOKONA, TOO!!
HUGG
THAT THING EVEN STARTLED ME!
I MEAN, THAT KUDAN IS BIG!
HUGG

KWOOOM
H-HEY, I'M ALL RIGHT! I'M JUST FINE!
GO BACK TO *NORMAL* ALREADY!
DOOOM
WHAT'S WRONG WITH THAT KUDAN?
DOOOM
THE FEATHER HAD TOO MUCH POWER FOR IT.
THAT'S MORE KUDAN THAN MASA-YOSHI CAN CONTROL.
WAFFT
STOP IT!!
WHAT'LL YOU DO NOW?
SHHP

I'M GOING TO GET SAKURA'S FEATHER BACK.
HOW DO YOU INTEND TO FIGHT SOMETHING THAT BIG?
ONE SLIP UP AND YOU'RE DEAD!
I WON'T DIE.
I STILL HAVE SOME-THING TO SEE THROUGH.
I CAN'T DIE YET.

MM.
COUNT ON KURO-PI TO HANDLE THINGS HERE.
YOU GO AHEAD.
EH?!
WHAT DO YOU MEAN, ME?!
THEN I'LL SEE YOU LATER.

WHOOSH
SYAORAN-KUN HAS STRENGTH.
IN A LOT OF DIFFERENT WAYS.
DOOOM
I GET THE FEELING THAT I UNDERSTAND...
...WHY THAT FIRE KUDAN CAME TO HIM.

STOP!!
I TOLD YOU TO STOP!!
GWOOOO
GLTTR
GLTTR
IT'S SPARKLING.
WOBBL
D-DOOM
DOOM
GASP
TMP
SYAORAN-KUN!!

I TOLD YOU THAT THERE WAS SOME-THING I WAS LOOKING FOR.
NOW...
...I'VE FOUND IT INSIDE OF YOUR KUDAN.
Y—
YOU MEAN *THIS?!*
WHOOM
I NEED TO GET IT BACK.

BUT...
MY KUDAN ISN'T LISTENING TO A WORD I SAY!
WHOOOSH
SYAORAN-KUN!
IF YOU GET TOO CLOSE, IT'LL—
ZUWHOOM

GHOOOOOH
GUGURK
MY KUDAN IS SPOUTING FIRE!!
STOP IT!!
YOU'LL KILL SYAORAN-KUN!!

ZHUUUUUUUUU
YOU'LL KILL SYAORAN-KUN!
SHUU
SHUU
ZLOOB
ZLOOB
YOU'LL KILL HIM!!

SYAORAN-KUN!
FWAAA
SYAORAN-KUN!
H-HOT!!
AH!

GHOOOOH
MASAYOSHI-KUN!
URRNG!
T— TAKE IT!!
IF THE THING INSIDE MY KUDAN IS THE THING YOU'RE LOOKING FOR...
...THEN I WANT YOU TO HAVE IT!
KRKL
KRKL
SO IF IT BURNS ME, LET IT BURN!!

SHHHHHHHHHH
THE LEAST I COULD DO WAS KEEP THE PLACE FROM CATCHING FIRE.

PAAA
SAKURA'S FEATHER!
SAKURA'S MEMORY!
I WAS ABLE...
...TO GET ONE BACK FOR HER!

Chapitre.13
The Reason for Tears

IT'S GOTTEN CLOUDY.
I WONDER IF IT'LL TURN INTO A SHOWER.
TMP TMP TMP
WELCOME HOME, SYAORAN!
HOW'D IT GO?
TMP
TWRL
WAZZAT?
I SEE YOU'RE IN SOMETHING OF A HURRY.
BUT WHY DO YOU LOOK LIKE A DIRTY CINDER?
I FOUND ONE OF SAKURA'S FEATHERS!
YOU DID?!

BAKAM
PAAAAAA
WITH THIS FEATHER... PLEASE WAKE UP!
SAKURA!!

"IF I FALL ASLEEP LIKE THIS..."
"...THE FIRST THING I'LL SEE WHEN I WAKE UP..."
PAAA
"...WILL BE YOU, SYAORAN."
GRMP

MNN
SAKURA!!

.....
WHO...

...ARE YOU?

I'M CALLED SYAORAN.
AND YOU... ...ARE HER HIGHNESS, PRINCESS SAKURA.

IF YOU'D BE SO KIND AS TO LISTEN, I'LL EXPLAIN.
YOU ARE A PRINCESS FROM ANOTHER WORLD.
ANOTHER... WORLD?
AND AT THE MOMENT, YOU'VE LOST YOUR MEMORY. IT'S IN ORDER TO FIND YOUR MEMORIES THAT YOU'RE TRAVELING BETWEEN WORLDS.
PAK
PAK
BY MYSELF?
NO...
YOU HAVE TRAVELING COMPANIONS.
ARE YOU... ONE OF THOSE?
YES.

YOU'RE DOING THIS FOR A TOTAL STRANGER?
I AM.
SST
PRINCESS SAKURA, I'M PLEASED TO MAKE YOUR ACQUAINTANCE.
FAI D. FLOWRIGHT AT YOUR SERVICE.
DMP

AND MAY I PRESENT—
I'M KURO-GANE.
NICE TA MEETCHA!
SHAKE!
AND THIS CUTE, FLUFFY ONE IS...
SHUPP
しゅたっ
MOKONA MODOKI! BUT YOU CAN SAY MOKONA!

SHHHHHHHHHHHHHHH

AT THAT MOMENT, I WAS SURE…
…HE WOULD CRY.
IT SEEMS THAT SAKURA-CHAN IS THE MOST IMPORTANT PERSON IN THE WORLD TO SYAORAN-KUN.
SO WHEN SHE SAID, "WHO ARE YOU?" I FELT CERTAIN HE WOULD CRY.
I WONDER IF HE'S CRYING NOW.
DON'T KNOW.
BUT IF HE WANTS TO KEEP FROM CRYING, HE'LL JUST HAVE TO GET STRONGER.
STRONG ENOUGH SO THAT *HE* WON'T BE THE ONE CRYING IN THE END.

YEAH...
BUT...
FWAFF
I ALSO THINK THERE'S A CERTAIN STRENGTH THAT'S NEEDED TO BE ABLE TO CRY WHEN YOU SHOULD.

WHILE I WAS SLEEPING, I WONDER IF SOME-ONE WAS HOLDING MY HAND...
MY HAND...
...FELT JUST SO NICE AND WARM!

IT SEEMS ONE OF THE FEATHERS HAS BEEN RETURNED TO HER.
YES.
BUT IN THE PATHS TO COME, THERE IS NO GUARANTEE THAT THEY WILL BE AS LUCKY AS THEY WERE THIS TIME.

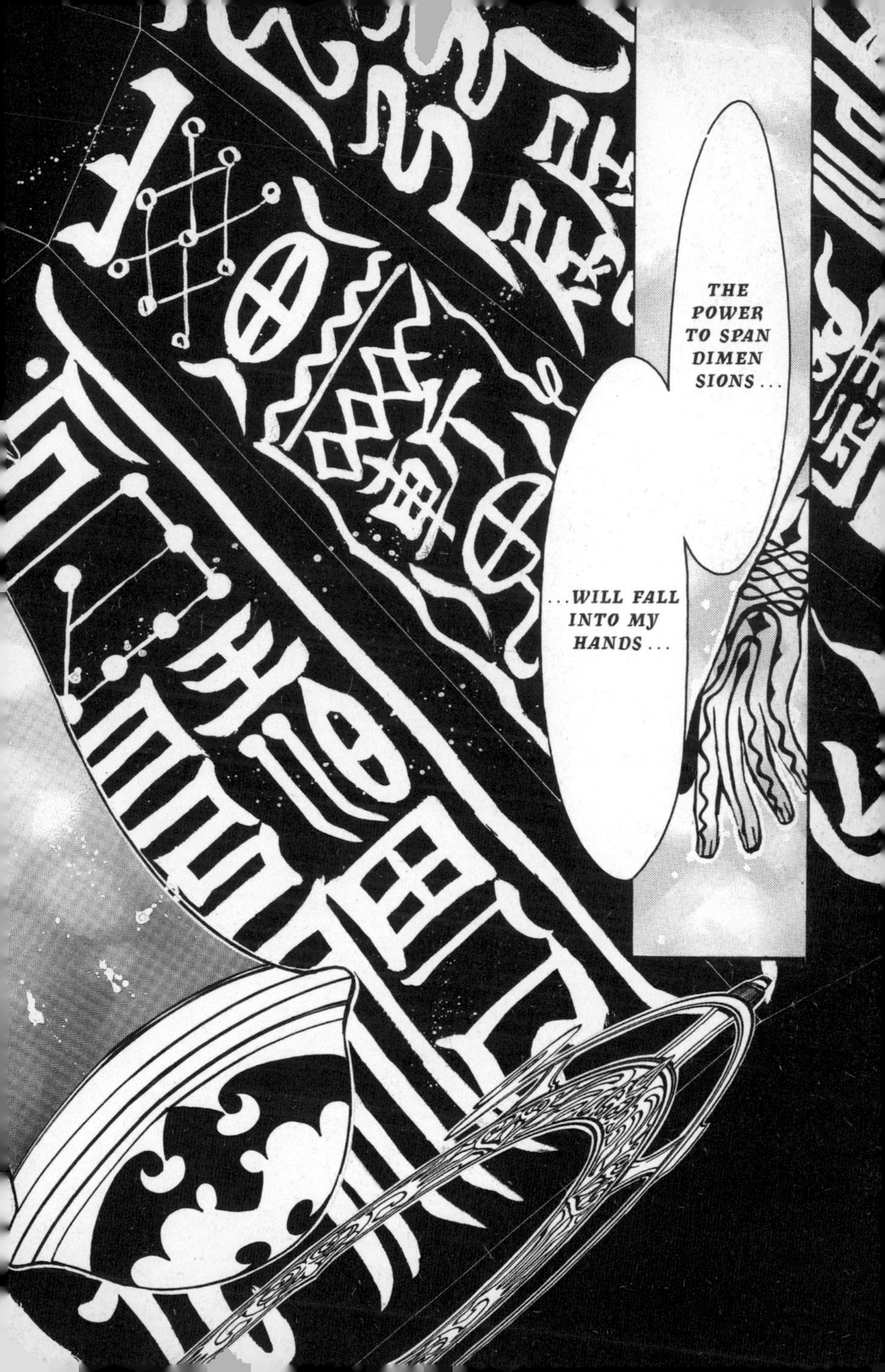
THE POWER TO SPAN DIMEN SIONS . . .
. . .WILL FALL INTO MY HANDS . . .

...NO MATTER HOW MUCH BLOOD NEEDS TO SPILL TO MAKE IT HAPPEN!

About the Creators

CLAMP is a group of four women who have become the most popular manga artists in The United Kingdom—Ageha Ohkawa, Mokona, Satsuki Igarashi, and Tsubaki Nekoi. They started out as doujinshi (fan comics) creators, but their skill and craft brought them to the attention of publishers very quickly. Their first work from a major publisher was *RG Veda*, but their first mass success was with *Magic Knight Rayearth*. From there, they went on to write many series, including *Cardcaptor Sakura* and *Chobits*, two of the most popular manga available. Like many Japanese manga artists, they prefer to avoid the spotlight, and little is known about them personally.

CLAMP is currently publishing three series in Japan: *Tsubasa* and *xxxHOLiC* with Kodansha and *Gohou Drug* with Kadokawa.

Past Works

CLAMP have created many series. Here is a brief overview of one of them.

X/1999

Kamui Shirou left Tokyo after the death of the mother of his friends, Fuma and Kotori. Now, six years later, Kamui is confronted by a vision of his own mother's death. Burning, she commands him to seek his destiny in Tokyo, and so he returns.

A turning point for the planet Earth is coming in the year 1999. Ravaged by mankind's carelessness, the planet is polluted and near death. The priestess Hinoto has seen two possible visions for humanity: In one, mankind is saved, and in the other, mankind is destroyed so that the earth can be born anew. The Seven Seals, or Dragons of Heaven, are pledged to fight for the preservation of humanity. The Seven Minions, or Dragons of Earth, want to exterminate all human life to make way for a new age.

Hinoto's vision centers on Kamui, who has the power to choose the world's fate. Pledged to protect his childhood friends Fuma and Kotori, Kamui finds allies in the form of Arashi and Sorata, two of the Seven Seals. (You've already met the Hanshin-reality versions of Arashi and Sorata (Sora) in *Tsubasa* volume 1.) For the sake of his friends, Kamui chooses to fight for the Seven Seals. Sadly, Fuma is Kamui's "twin star," his opposite number, and because Kamui chose the side of good for himself, Fuma is forced to join the side of evil, the Seven Minions. Thus Kamui must fight the friend he sought to save.

Acknowledged as one of CLAMP's most visually stunning manga, *X/1999* is set in the same world as *CLAMP School Detectives* and *Tokyo Babylon*, and is still an ongoing series. The manga has been adapted as an anime film and a TV series.

Translation Notes

Japanese is a tricky language for most Westerners, and translation is often more art than science. For your edification and reading pleasure, here are notes on some of the places where we could have gone in a different direction in our translation of the work, or where a Japanese cultural reference is used.

Kyaa!
"Kyaaaa" is standard onomatopoeia (sound word) for a scream in manga, but many Japanese people have adopted this sound and use it to express joy, surprise, and other happy emotions.

Tsuruhashi
The town in which our heroes stop by to eat okonomiyaki (see next entry) is called Tsuruhashi. In our world, Tsuruhashi is only about a kilometer south of Osaka Castle, and it is the station which connects the Osaka Loop Line that circles the city with the Kintetsu-Nara line which goes out to the suburbs between Osaka and Nara. Millions of people pass through this station, and because of that, it's only natural that the restaurants there are both famous and good!

Okonomiyaki

They call it Japanese pancakes or Japanese pizza, but the only thing similar between those and okonomiyaki is that all are round and flat. Okonomiyaki is made of flour, water, cabbage (mixed with other veggies), egg, seasonings, some kind of meat (seafood is common), and a delicious steak-sauce-like okonomiyaki sauce. The "konomi" means "like" or "love," and it indicates that you can put the veggies or meat you most like in it. The "yaki" means fried (the same as with "teriyaki" or "sukiyaki").

Flipping Rights

Most okonomiyaki that you will find in Japan is made in the kitchen, or at least, behind the counter. However, there are okonomiyaki restaurants where you can flip the okonomiyaki yourself. But since the dish was created in the Kansai (Osaka, Kyoto, Nara, Kobe) region, chefs jealously guard the right to flip their okonomiyaki—only when it's ready. After all, they are proud of their food and want it to be perfectly cooked.

Attack Names

Most anime, manga, and game fans are familiar with the attack names that the opponents shout at each other when making their attacks. Sure, it doesn't happen in real life, but it is a long-time entertainment convention. CLAMP was having a little crabby fun with the names of the attacks in this sequence.

I THINK IF YOU TRY TO GET INVOLVED, HE'LL GET REALLY MAD.
KURO-TAN'S LIKE THAT.

Kuro-tan

The pet names that Fai always chooses for Kurogane aren't actually honorifics. Although they are similar in meaning to -chan, they are usually invented by young women who want to appear cute and add cute sounds to the names of people in their inner circle (close female friends and boyfriends). These syllables make the name sound almost babylike, and so Fai giving those names to gruff Kurogane is massively inappropriate, and as such, very funny.

THEY HATE LOSING; THEY NEVER GET TO THE POINT; THEY'LL ATTACK IF YOU'RE NOT PAYING ATTENTION; IF OUR TEAM WINS THEY GO CRAZY; THEY THROW THEMSELVES IN THE RIVER . . .

Drawbacks to Hanshin's People

Sorata's list of complaints about the people of the Hanshin Republic are common conceptions that Tokyoites have for the people of Osaka. Their stand-up comedy is famous for a Laurel and Hardy dynamic where one person says something dumb, and the other hits him over the head for it. And yes, they do throw themselves into the dirty, polluted river when the Hanshin Tigers win the national championship.

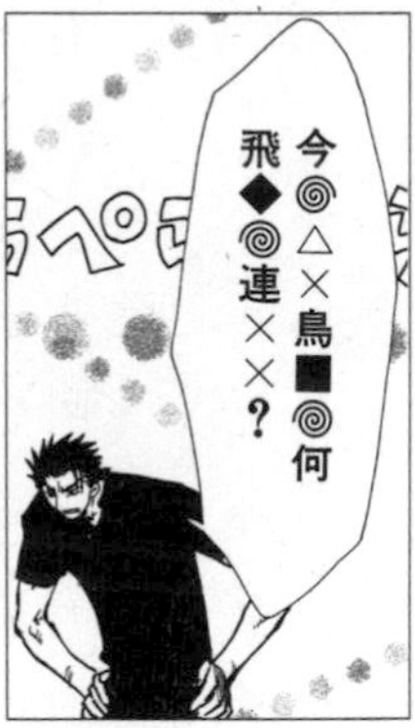

Kurogane's Language

Students of Chinese or Japanese may be able to make some sense out of Kurogane's language. The kanji in his word balloons are real, and if you look them up, you should be able to get some idea of what he is saying.

We Have a Winner!

The original sound effect here was "Pin-pon, pin-pon," the universal sound (in Japan) for a correct answer in a quiz show.

Primera's Legion of Fans
Yes, CLAMP's depiction of Primera's fans is an exaggeration, but not by all that much...

"Is Everyone Having Fun?"
The Japanese phrase here is actually "Minna genki?" Similar to "Hello, Cleveland!" this is a standard phrase for a singer to say as a concert is beginning.

Tongue Twister 1
Like English, Japanese has a large variety of tongue twisters, and here some of the more famous are misquoted by Primera. "Tonari no Kyaku wa yoku kaki kuu kyaku da" ("The guest next door eats a lot of persimmon"). But Primera said, "Tonari no gaki wa yoku kyaku kuu gaki da" ("The brat next door eats a lot of guests").

THE SIXTH SHEIK'S *SICKO'S SHIP'S SUNK!*

Tongue Twister 2

The tongue twister Primela wanted to say was, "Nama-mugi, nama-gome, nama-tamago" ("Raw barley, raw rice, raw egg"), but she got one word wrong. "Nama-gome" became "Nama-gomi" ("Raw garbage").

RED LORRY, YELLOW LORRY, RED LORRY, YELLOW *YORRY!*

Tongue Twister 3

Primela tried to say, "Aka maki-gami, ao maki-gami, ki maki-gami" ("Red rolled paper, blue rolled paper, yellow rolled paper"), but she stumbled over the last words so it came out, "Maki-maki" ("rolled rolled").

A FLEA AND A FLY FLEW UP IN A FLUE, EE-AI-EE-AI-OH!

Tongue Twister 4

Primela was out of tongue twisters at this point, and she just started stringing words together like "pond skater," "red," and "aeiou."

"Call me idiot!"

The word for fool, "baka," that many fans know already, is Tokyo dialect. A different word for fool, "aho," is Osaka dialect. Oddly, "aho" is not terribly insulting in Osaka, but "baka" is, and the opposite is true in Tokyo. In the Japanese version, Primela called Shôgo "baka," and Shôgo replied, "At least say, 'Aho'!" He was noting that Primela was getting away from her Hanshin roots by using the word "baka."

SHÔGO-KUN, ALL YOU CARE ABOUT ARE YOUR KUDAN BATTLES! YOU RETARD!
DON'T SAY "RETARD"!
CALL ME A "FOOL" OR AN "IDIOT" IF YOU LIKE.

Preview of

TSUBASA

CLAMP

We are pleased to present to you a preview from Volume 3 available now from Tanoshimi.

GOWRRRRRR
THANK YOU!

WHAT'S THIS?
A LOT OF PEOPLE THERE!
GABASSH

カラッ
KRMBL
GLANCE
キョロ

FREE
wallpapers
icons
previews
downloads
competitions
visit
www.tanoshimi.tv
tanoshimi

TOMARE!!
STOP!!
YOU'RE GOING THE WRONG WAY!
MANGA IS A COMPLETELY DIFFERENT TYPE OF READING EXPERIENCE.
TO START AT THE BEGINNING, GO TO THE END!
THAT'S RIGHT! AUTHENTIC MANGA IS READ THE TRADITIONAL JAPANESE WAY—FROM RIGHT TO LEFT. EXACTLY THE OPPOSITE OF HOW ENGLISH BOOKS ARE READ. IT'S EASY TO FOLLOW: JUST GO TO THE OTHER END OF THE BOOK, AND READ EACH PAGE—AND EACH PANEL—FROM THE RIGHT SIDE TO THE LEFT SIDE, STARTING AT THE TOP RIGHT. NOW YOU'RE EXPERIENCING MANGA AS IT WAS MEANT TO BE.